Symbols of Canada

Flags

Edited by Deborah Lambert

Weigl

Published by Weigl Educational Publishers Limited
6325 10 Street SE
Calgary, Alberta
T2H 2Z9

www.weigl.com

Library and Archives Canada Cataloguing in Publication data available upon request.
Fax 403-233-7769 for the attention of the Publishing Records department.

ISBN 978-1-55388-921-2 (hard cover)
ISBN 978-1-55388-927-4 (soft cover)

Printed in the United States of America
1 2 3 4 5 6 7 8 9 0   13 12 11 10 09

Editor: Heather C. Hudak
Design: Kathryn Livingstone

All of the Internet URLs given in the book were valid at the time of publication. However, due to the dynamic nature
of the Internet, some addresses may have changed, or sites may have ceased to exist since publication. While the author
and publisher regret any inconvenience this may cause readers, no responsibility for any such changes can be accepted
by either the author or the publisher.

Every reasonable effort has been made to trace ownership and to obtain permission to reprint copyright material. The publishers
would be pleased to have any errors or omissions brought to their attention so that they may be corrected in subsequent printings.

Weigl acknowledges Getty Images as one of its image suppliers for this title.

We gratefully acknowledge the financial support of the Government of Canada through the Book Publishing Industry Development
Program (BPIDP) for our publishing activities.

Contents

Ontario

Northwest Territories

Saskatchewan

Prince Edward Island

Nunavut

Quebec

Yukon

What are Symbols?

A symbol is an item that stands for something else. Objects, artworks, or living things can all be symbols. Every Canadian province and territory has official symbols. These items represent the people, history, and culture of the provinces and territories. Symbols of the provinces and territories create feelings of pride and citizenship among the people who live there. A flag is a type of emblem. Each of the ten provinces and three territories has an official flag. This is one of many symbols a province or territory can have.

Creating the National Flag

The first Canadian flag designs were made in 1925 but were never used. In 1946, the Canadian Parliament asked citizens to create more design ideas. It received about 2,600 designs, but a flag was still not chosen. Prime Minister Lester B. Pearson called for even more flag designs in 1964. The choice was narrowed to three designs. The flag selected was designed by Jacques St. Cyr. Canada's flag was first raised at noon on February 15, 1965, in an official ceremony on Parliament Hill.

The Red Ensign was the flag of Canada prior to the current design.

Locating Provinces and Territories

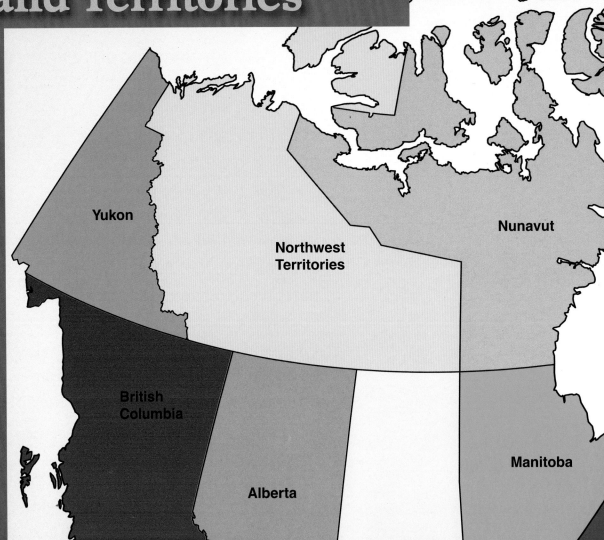

Yukon

Northwest Territories

Nunavut

British Columbia

Alberta

Saskatchewan

Manitoba

Each province and territory has a flag. Each province and territory is unique because of its land, people, and wildlife. Throughout this book, the provinces and regions are colour coded. To find a flag, first find the province or territory using the map on this page. Then, turn to the pages that have the same colour province or territory image in the top corner.

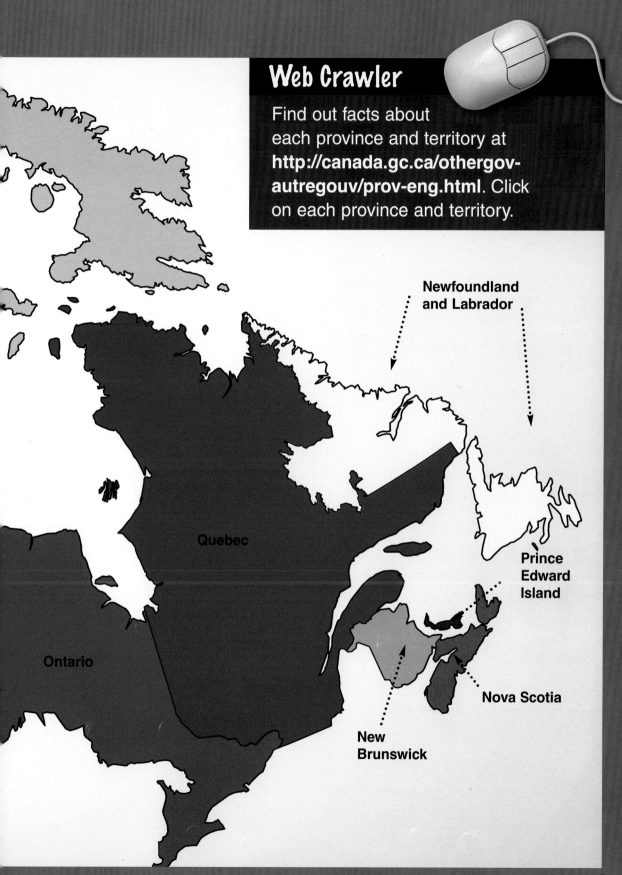

Web Crawler

Find out facts about each province and territory at **http://canada.gc.ca/othergov-autregouv/prov-eng.html**. Click on each province and territory.

Newfoundland and Labrador

Quebec

Prince Edward Island

Ontario

Nova Scotia

New Brunswick

Canada's Land and People

Canada is a large country. The ten Canadian provinces and three territories cover a vast amount of land. From one province or territory to another, the people, lifestyles, land, and animals are quite different. Each province and territory has its own identity. As a united country, Canada also has its own identity. Canada uses emblems to represent this identity.

Nova Scotia

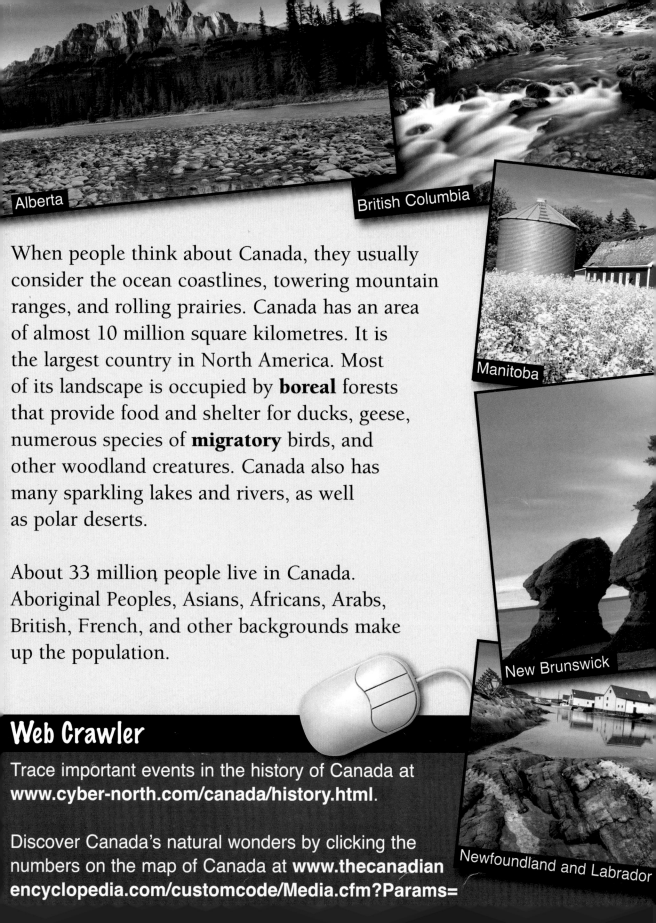

Alberta

British Columbia

Manitoba

New Brunswick

Newfoundland and Labrador

When people think about Canada, they usually consider the ocean coastlines, towering mountain ranges, and rolling prairies. Canada has an area of almost 10 million square kilometres. It is the largest country in North America. Most of its landscape is occupied by **boreal** forests that provide food and shelter for ducks, geese, numerous species of **migratory** birds, and other woodland creatures. Canada also has many sparkling lakes and rivers, as well as polar deserts.

About 33 million people live in Canada. Aboriginal Peoples, Asians, Africans, Arabs, British, French, and other backgrounds make up the population.

Web Crawler

Trace important events in the history of Canada at **www.cyber-north.com/canada/history.html**.

Discover Canada's natural wonders by clicking the numbers on the map of Canada at **www.thecanadian encyclopedia.com/customcode/Media.cfm?Params=**

Alberta

Alberta's provincial flag became official on June 1, 1968. In its present design, a **shield**, taken from Alberta's **coat of arms**, appears in the middle of the flag on a blue background. This blue colour used for the background is referred to as "Alberta blue." It was adopted as one of the provincial colours in 1984 and represents Alberta's bright, blue skies.

At the top of the shield is the Cross of St. George. This cross, placed on a white background, represents King George III and symbolizes Alberta's links to Great Britain. On the bottom of the shield lies a landscape with mountains, hills, a prairie, and a wheat field. The scene depicts the landscape of the province. The gold colour used for the wheat field is called "Alberta gold." Like Alberta blue, this colour was adopted as one of the provincial colours in 1984.

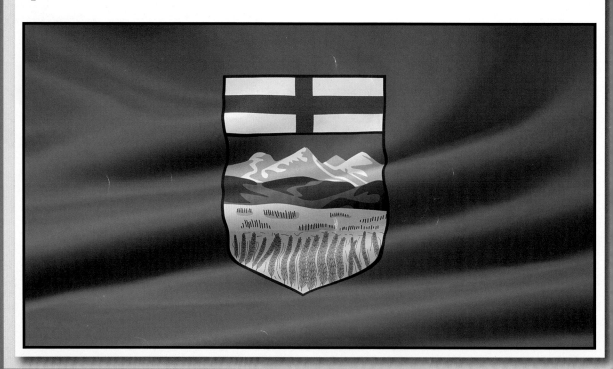

British Columbia

British Columbia's provincial flag was adopted on June 27, 1960. The flag's design copies the shield on the province's coat of arms. Great Britain's flag, the **Union Jack**, is on the top half of the shield. A crown sits at the center of the Union Jack. Both the flag and crown represent British Columbia's past as a colony of Great Britain.

The Sun and wavy blue make up the bottom part of the shield. The Sun symbolizes the glory of the province. It also represents the fact that British Columbia is the most western province in Canada. The wavy blue lines symbolize the Pacific Ocean. The Sun and wavy blue lines show British Columbia's location between the Rocky Mountains and the Pacific Ocean.

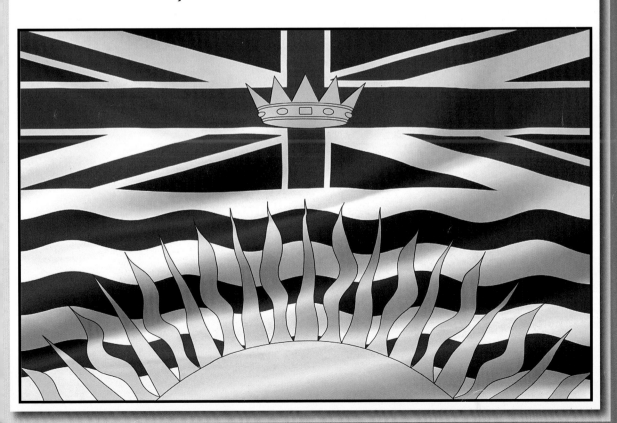

Manitoba

Manitoba's provincial flag was given royal approval by Her Majesty Queen Elizabeth II in October 1965. It was proclaimed as the official flag on May 12, 1966.

Before the provincial flag was approved, the province used the Union Jack. In 1964, the provincial government decided to design its own flag based on the Red Ensign. The province included the Union Jack in the upper left corner of the flag.

The province's shield is on the right half of the flag. The Cross of St. George appears on the top part of the shield. Under the cross, a bison symbolizes the vast herds that once roamed throughout the province. These herds provided food and clothing to Aboriginal Peoples and early settlers.

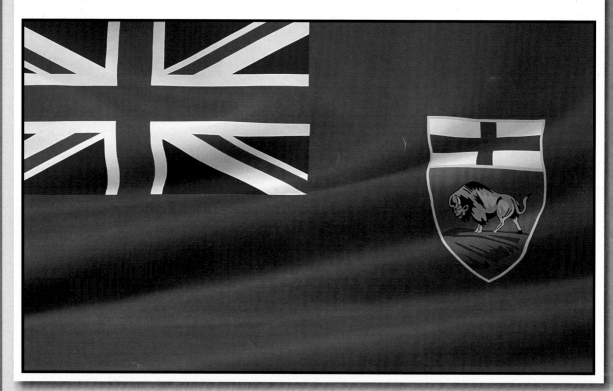

New Brunswick

The provincial flag of New Brunswick was adopted by **proclamation** on February 24, 1965. The symbols on the flag were taken from the **armorial bearing**s. These were granted to New Brunswick in 1868 by Queen Victoria.

A gold lion appears against a red background on the top part of the flag. This lion connects the province to the royal family of Brunswick-Lüneberg, for which it was named.

Beneath the lion, a ship with moving oars occupies the bottom part of the shield. It represents the province's shipping past. The wavy blue lines below the ship link the province to the sea.

Newfoundland and Labrador

Newfoundland and Labrador's provincial flag was designed by Christopher Pratt, an artist born in St. John's. It became the official flag on May 28, 1980.

The white background on the flag stands for the ice and snow of the tundra. The blue color represents the sea. The red symbolizes human effort, and gold represents the bright future ahead.

The blue section resembles the left half of the Union Jack. It represents the province's **Commonwealth** history. The two red triangles symbolize the province's mainland and the island. The gold arrow shows the province's hope for the future. Together with the triangles, it forms a **trident**. This symbolizes the province's dependence on fishing and the sea.

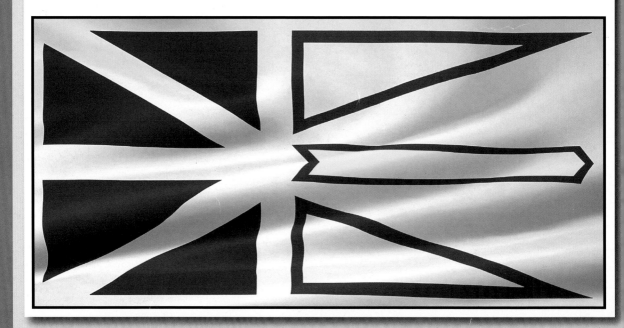

Northwest Territories

The flag of the Northwest Territories was designed by Robert Bessant from Margaret, Manitoba. It became the official flag on January 1, 1969.

In the present design of the flag, the territorial shield is centred on a white background, representing the ice and snow of the North. On the shield, white represents polar ice. The wavy blue line symbolizes the **Northwest Passage**.

The red on the lower part of the shield shows the territory's northern tundra. The fox's head is a symbol of the many animals found in the area. Green stands for the forests found in the southern parts of the territory, while the gold bars symbolize minerals. The blue bars on each side of the white background represent the territory's many lakes and rivers.

Nova Scotia

The flag of Nova Scotia was the first flag in the Commonwealth to be authorized by **Royal Charter** in 1625. It was officially adopted in 1929, more than 300 years after the design was approved. The flag copies the design of Nova Scotia's shield. It is one of the simplest flags in the country.

Nova Scotia's flag is similar to the Scottish flag, only reversed. The Scottish flag has a white **saltire** on a blue background. In its present design, Nova Scotia's flag has a white background with a blue "X" across the centre. The "X" stands for the Cross of Saint Andrew, the patron saint of Scotland. In the centre of the "X" is the Royal Lion. It is set within a double red border on a yellow or gold background. The Royal Lion is a symbol of Scottish royalty.

Nunavut

Nunavut's provincial flag was unveiled on April 1, 1999. People across Canada were invited to submit design ideas. A committee of elders and artists analyzed the submissions and selected 10 finalists. The flag was designed using ideas from each finalist.

An inukshuk stands in the centre of Nunavut's flag. An inukshuk is a pile of stones that is meant to resemble a person. The red colour of the inukshuk on the flag shows Nunavut's connection to Canada. Niqirtsuituq, or the North Star, is in the top right corner of the flag. It represents the leadership of community elders. The North Star and the inukshuk have guided the Inuit people across the frozen trails of their homeland for centuries. The blue and gold on the flag symbolize the riches of the land, the sea, and the sky.

Ontario

The provincial flag of Ontario received royal approval on April 14, 1965, and was proclaimed on May 21. As part of its design, the flag has a solid red background.

The Union Jack appears in the flag's top left corner. The Union Jack represents the close relationship between Ontario and Great Britain. In the bottom right corner of Ontario's flag is the provincial shield. This is the same shield found on the province's official coat of arms.

The top of the shield shows the Cross of St. George. This cross represents the British **heritage** of many people in Ontario. It also honours King George III, who ruled the colony when the shield was created. Three golden maple leaves on a green background represent the common maple trees found in the province.

Prince Edward Island

Prince Edward Island's flag became official on March 24, 1964. It was created as part of the 100th anniversary of the **Charlottetown Conference**.

The flag's design is based on the province's shield. It has a lion, which is a symbol of Great Britain, on a red background. Beneath the lion is a plot of grass representing Prince Edward Island and England. An oak tree, the official tree of Prince Edward Island, stands on the grass. Since 1767, Prince Edward Island has been divided into three counties. These are Kings county, Queens county, and Prince county. The three smaller saplings on the left of the oak tree symbolize these counties. The bands of red and white on the top, bottom, and right side of the flag represent Canada's official colours.

Quebec

Quebec was the first province to officially adopt a provincial flag. It was adopted on January 21, 1948, and is often called the "fleur-de-lis" flag.

Quebec's flag shows a white cross on a blue background. The cross honours old French military flags. The bars of the cross divide the flag into four sections. A white fleur-de-lis appears in the centre of each section. These flowers have represented the kings of France since about 1000 A.D. The fleur-de-lis has become a symbol of Quebec.

This flag was made Quebec's official emblem in 1999. It is flown on the central tower of the Parliament Building in Quebec City, as well as other sites throughout the province.

Saskatchewan

Saskatchewan's provincial flag was officially dedicated on September 22, 1969. It was based on a design by Anthony Drake, who had won a provincial flag design competition.

Saskatchewan's flag consists of two horizontal halves. Green stands for the province's forests and grass, and yellow represents its wheat fields.

The western red lily is on the right side of the flag. It is the province's official flower.

The provincial shield of arms is in the upper left corner. The top of the shield features the red royal lion. The lion represents Saskatchewan's links to England. Three golden sheaves of wheat on a green background are displayed on the bottom of the shield.

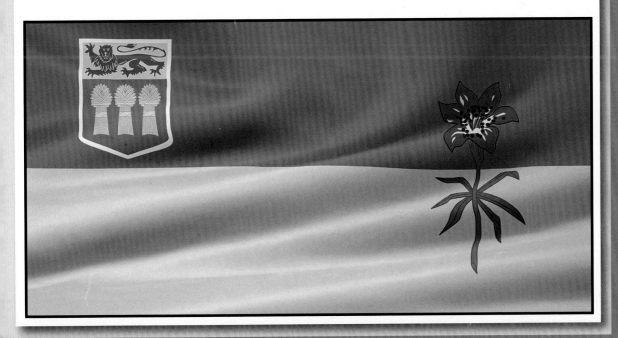

Yukon

Yukon's flag was adopted on December 1, 1967. The Royal Canadian Legion's Whitehorse branch held a competition as part of Canada's 100th birthday celebrations. Lynn Lambert created the winning design.

The green panel symbolizes the Yukon's forests. White represents snow, and blue is for lakes and rivers. In the centre, the coat of arms is supported by fireweed, the Yukon's official flower.

The Cross of St. George at the top of the shield represents English explorers. The "roundel in vair," or circle with fur, in the centre of the cross stands for the fur trade. Red triangles on the bottom of the shield represent the territory's mountains. Gold circles are a symbol of minerals. Wavy white and blue lines show the Yukon River and Klondike creeks where gold was found. The Malamute dog represents this animal's importance as a link to survival in the hostile wilderness of the Yukon.

Guide to Flags

THE NATIONAL FLAG

ALBERTA

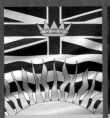

BRITISH COLUMBIA

MANITOBA

NEW BRUNSWICK

NEWFOUNDLAND AND LABRADOR

NORTHWEST TERRITORIES

NOVA SCOTIA

NUNAVUT

ONTARIO

PRINCE EDWARD ISLAND

QUEBEC

SASKATCHEWAN

YUKON

Canada's National Flag

National emblems are symbols that are used for the entire country. The national animal, the beaver, is one such symbol. Another is the common loon, which is the national bird. The maple is the national tree. The Canadian flag, known as the Maple Leaf, is the national flag.

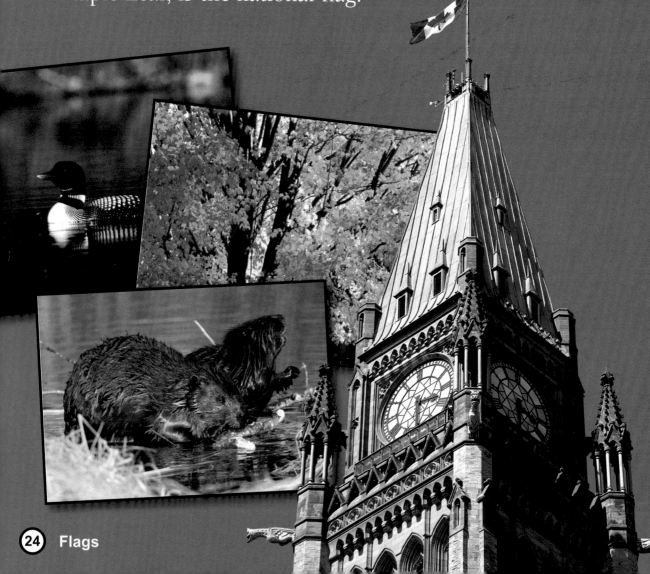

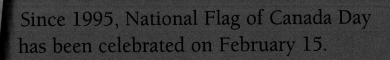

Since 1995, National Flag of Canada Day has been celebrated on February 15.

The inspiration for a red and white flag came from Dr. George Stanley, Dean of Arts at the Royal Military College in Kingston, Ontario.

According to the Honourable Maurice Bourget, Speaker of the Senate, "The flag is the symbol of the nation's unity, for it, beyond any doubt, represents all the citizens of Canada without distinction of race, language, belief or opinion."

Coat of Arms History

At the time of **Confederation**, Canada's flag was the Union Jack. After much debate about the design of the national flag, on October 29, 1964, it was recommended to the House of Commons that the red and white maple leaf design be adopted. The National Flag of Canada was proclaimed by Queen Elizabeth II on January 28, 1965. It took effect on February 15, 1965.

Parts of the National Flag

Canada's national flag is one of the most symbolically important emblems in the country.

MAPLE LEAF The maple leaf has served as a symbol celebrating the nature and environment of what is now Canada since the 1700s. On the national flag, it is a **stylized** 11-point red leaf. The number of points on this leaf have no special significance. The size of the flag was outlined by Mr. George Bist, a World War II veteran, and the precise colouration of the flag was defined by Dr. Gunter Wyszechi.

COLOURS Red and white were approved as Canada's official colours in the proclamation of the royal arms of Canada in 1921 by King George V.

PANELS The red panels represent **valour** and strength.

WHITE BACKGROUND The white background represents purity and innocence.

Test Your Knowledge

1 What is the Canadian Red Ensign?

4 Which provincial flag became official on June 1, 1968?

2 Who designed the national flag?

5 When were the first Canadian flag designs made?

3 When did the national flag become official?

6 What does the blue panel on the Yukon flag represent?

7 In which provincial flag does red represent human effort?

8 What does the Cross of St. George represent?

9 What is the provincial flower of Saskatchewan?

13 Which flag became an official emblem in 1999?

10 What are Canada's official colours?

14 Who is Robert Bessant?

11 Which provincial flag was approved more than 300 years after it was designed?

15 What is the Northwest Passage?

12 What country does the fleur-de-lis represent?

Answers:

1. A red flag with the Union Jack in the upper corner
2. Jacques St. Cyr
3. February 15, 1965
4. Alberta's
5. 1925
6. Lakes and rivers
7. Newfoundland and Labrador
8. King George III and the provinces' British heritage
9. Western red lily
10. Red and white
11. Nova Scotia's
12. France
13. Quebec's
14. The man who designed the provincial flag of the Northwest Territories
15. A waterway that connects the Atlantic and Pacific Oceans

Create Your Own Flag

Create a flag to represent your community. Begin by thinking about your community's history. Use this book to help you. You may want to include your community's symbolic animals, trees, and flowers.

Think about how your flag will look. Will it have a shield? What colours will you include? How will you arrange the symbolic items on the shield? Why? Look at the pictures in this book for help.

Draw your flag on a piece of paper. Use the diagram on pages 26 and 27 to help you design the parts of your flag. Colour your drawing with felt markers. When you are finished, label the parts of your flag.

Write a description of your flag. What does each item or colour represent? What does it say about your community?

Further Research

Many books and websites provide information on Canada's flags. To learn more about these flags, borrow books from the library, or surf the Internet.

Books

Most libraries have computers that connect to a database for researching information. If you input a key word, you will be provided with a list of books in the library that contain information on that topic. Nonfiction books are arranged numerically, using their call number. Fiction books are organized alphabetically by the author's last name.

Websites

Find fun facts about each of Canada's provinces and territories at **www.pco-bcp.gc.ca/aia/index.asp?lang=eng&page=provterr&sub=map-carte&doc=map-carte-eng.htm**.

Learn about Canada's flags and other symbols at **www.patrimoinecanadien.gc.ca/pgm/ceem-cced/symbl/index-eng.cfm**.

To practise drawing the flags of Canada, visit **www.uptoten.com/kids/boowakwala-events-flag-activity.html**.

Glossary

armorial bearings: another name for coat of arms

boreal: northern regions with very cold temperatures

Charlottetown Conference: a conference that led to the creation of Canada

coat of arms: a design belonging to a particular person or group of people and used by them in a wide variety of ways

Commonwealth: countries that were part of the British Empire

Confederation: a union of states or groups

heritage: something handed down from earlier generations

migratory: to move from one place to another

Northwest Passage: a waterway that connects the Atlantic and Pacific Oceans

proclamation: a formal public statement

Royal Charter: an official document granted by the sovereign

saltire: a term used for St. Andrew's Cross

shield: a decorative emblem that identifies an organization or government

stylized: shown in an unrealistic manner

trident: a tool used to hunt fish

Union Jack: the flag of Great Britain

valour: courage in the face of danger

Index